Magic Objects for Beginners

Magic Wands, Snake Rings, Spiritus Familiaris, Talismans and more

for Ptah

Contact: www.HarryEilenstein.de
Harry.Eilenstein@web.de
Harry Eilenstein at youtube

Production and publishing house: BoD – Books on Demand, Norderstedt

ISBN: 9783753490854

Table of Contents

I   Objects in Magic

In magic, as in cult and religion, there are a variety of objects that are used and that have magical properties. Often they are made in a special way or have a special symbolism.

The best known is certainly the magic wand, but also from magic rings, wizard robes, temples, consecrated statues and the like almost everyone has heard once.

At least since the magic rings in "Lord of the Rings" and the magic swords, cloaks, stones, wands, horcruxes etc. in "Harry Potter" the idea of magical objects with special properties is widely spread. Many of these ideas go back to the Celts and the Germanic tribes, in whose myths and legends they can be found in abundance.

Of course, the first question is whether there really are objects that have magical properties of their own … … … They do exist.

The second question then logically is how to find or make such items.

A wise third question would be what such items are useful for and whether there are any real benefits to possessing such items.

These three questions (and some aspects around them) will be explored in more detail in this book.

II General Symbolism

First of all, there are some magical objects that appear so frequently in myths and legends and also as real objects in archaeology that they can be taken as archetypes.

II 1. Traditional symbolism

Some of these magical objects can be attributed to religion, mythology and cult. This does not mean that they have no or particularly great magical properties – this only means that they are firmly embedded in a socio-religious context.

There are, of course, a great number of different traditions in which such objects appear: Judaism, Christianity, Islam, Hinduism, Buddhism, ancient Egypt, Germanic peoples, Celts, Siberian peoples, Voodoo, Mayans, Aztecs, Qetchua ("Incas"), Inuit ("Eskimos"), Bantus, etc.

Some symbols occur in practically all peoples and are therefore the basic symbols – also in magic.

In the following, of course, not all symbolic objects can be listed and considered, but only a small selection – but this selection will hopefully suffice for a solid basic understanding of "magical objects with traditional symbolism".

II 1. a) The sweat lodge

The oldest known magical object is the sweat lodge. It originated about 600,000 years ago when Homo erectus needed heated huts to survive in cold northern Eurasia during the Ice Age.

Unheated versions of these huts were in use as early as 1,900,000 years ago – some stone foundations of them have survived. They consisted of a flat, ring-shaped wall made of stones laid one on top of the other, on which a hemispherical roof made of branches and skins stood.

The heating system, invented 600,000 years ago, was simple: stones were made to glow in a fire in front of the hut, and then with the help of the shoulder blade bone of a hunted animal or similar were brought into a small pit in the center of the hut. If necessary one poured some water over the glowing stones, so that it became really hot in the hut.

These huts were probably already associated with the mother's belly at that time. So it didn't take much to not only associate them with the mother's belly, but to specifically focus on this "heated hut" to regain protection and basic trust – which gave rise to the sweat lodge ritual.

The first temples of man, built at the end of the Ice Age 12,000 years ago in northern Mesopotamia in Göbekli Tepe, still had the same shape: a circular wall with a hemispherical roof made of branches and skins. However, the image of the mother's belly was architecturally represented in much greater detail at that time:

- an outer stone ring with a roof = the mother's belly
- an inner stone ring with roof = the child in its mother's belly (where the ritual participants sat)
- a connecting wall between both rings = the umbilical cord
- a passage to the outer stone ring = the mother's vagina
- a stone plate with a hole in front of the stone ring = the entrance to the vagina

Five other elements were found in the temple, which are also well known from today's sweat lodges:

- mostly eight stylized people in the form of angular pillars = ancestors (in the simple sweat lodge these are the vertical rods in the sweat lodge frame)
- two pillars in the center of the inner stone circle = body and soul
- two panthers at the entrance = the animals of the Mother Goddess, who at that time has been also a hunter goddess (panther = the power and hunting success for the hunters of that time)
- animals as reliefs and statuettes = birds (souls), predators (power), gregarious animals (fertility), snakes (ancestors) – these animals are still found in today's sweat lodge rituals
- the mother goddess as a relief or a statuette = mother

These sweat lodge temples have been developed in many ways during the Neolithic period:

- to stone circles = the rectangular stone pillars in the inner stone circle of the temple became the menhir circles, the passage to the circle became the stone avenue, the two panthers at the entrance became the two large menhirs at the beginning of the stone avenue leading to the stone circle, the two large pillars in the middle of the inner circle (body and soul) became the two large pillars in the middle of the menhir circles

7

- to temples = the oldest temples were rooms to which a passage led ("passage temple")

- to mounds = the hemispherical temples with the passage to the interior became hemispherical mounds with a passage to the burial chamber in the interior

- to pyramids = the stone ring wall and the mound tomb became angular and the passage became the covered way leading from the valley temple to the pyramid (in the Egyptian pyramid version)

- to statues of gods = further development of the statues of the mother goddess, the ancestors and the animals

In later times, by leaving out the magical-religious aspects, the sweat lodge became the thermal baths, spas and saunas.

II 1. b) The magic wand

The second oldest known symbol is the bird stick. It was invented by Homo sapiens at least 100,000 years ago in his original homeland in Central Africa. It is possible, however, that this symbol is much older. It is found in all cultures. The oldest representation originates from the cave paintings in southern France 25,0000 years ago. In Göbekli Tepe, 12,000 years ago, bird sticks made of stone are found, which shows how important this symbol must have been at that time in the cult of the sweat lodge temples.

These symbols consist of a staff with a bird on top. They represent a human being (staff) and his soul (bird).

The soul is represented worldwide as a bird, a human being with a bird's head, a human being with a bird's robe, a bird with a human head, a human being with wings (angels), etc., because during a near-death one experiences that one leaves one's own body and floats above it and can consequently look at it from above ("astral travel"). Thereby one recognizes that the human being is more than only his body. That which one experiences in a near-death is apparently something that can hover and fly – it is thus "like a bird" and could thus best be represented as a bird: the soul bird.

These bird sticks then became the totem pole of the late Paleolithic period 50,000 years ago, when Homo sapiens met Homo erectus and Neanderthal man in Eurasia. This is simply a larger version of the bird pole: a tree trunk with a wooden bird perched on top.

Such a tree trunk invited to represent on it other symbolisms like the snakes

(Kundalini), the ancestors (skulls), the mother goddess etc.. Thus, already in the late Paleolithic period, totem poles with complex symbolism were created, which were made in the time of Göbekli Tepe of stone. There has been a variety of these stone totem poles in Göbekli Tepe, Nevali Cori and other places of this ancient culture.

These bird poles then became the first "religious scepters", which are found at Göbekli Tepe as the stone poles with bird heads. These were the first precursors of the "magic wands". It is possible that such bird wands already existed in the late Paleolithic period as a symbol of the shamans – possibly made of wood.

As an increasingly complex mythology developed in the Neolithic period to describe the world of the agriculturalists, which was much more complex than the world of the early hunters, the bird wand also evolved.

The staff was associated, among other things, with the world tree, which had been the link between heaven and earth. It was therefore the shaman's staff, the seer's staff and the magic staff – a sign that the bearer of this staff knew astral travel and was able to make a conscious contact with the gods and ancestors in the other world and successfully ask them for advice and help for the living.

The bird staff was a "portable world tree", a "portable totem pole".

In kingship, the bird staff became the scepter of kings, which represented the connection of the kings with the gods. The ancestral pillars in this era became the statues of the gods and the deceased, as well as the pillars in the temples.

The wands of the magicians have a long prehistory.

II 1. c) The skull

In magic today, skulls are mostly associated with black magic. However, since the Neolithic Age at the latest, there has been a tradition of keeping the skulls of the deceased in a niche in the wall of the dwelling house, in order to be able to contact the dead with the help of these skulls. Sometimes these skulls have been coverd with clay and painted to produce an image of the dead that was as naturlistic as possible.

From this tradition originate, among others, the cult of the dead, the spiritualistic sessions and the systemic family constellations.

Until medieval Christianity, there was a tradition of drinking from the skulls of special deceased persons, such as saints, in order to receive a blessing from them. In Tibetan Buddhism, this tradition still exists today.

From this custom derives the mythological motif of the talking skulls, known especially from the Celts (Bran), the Germanic tribes (Tyr-Mimir) and the Greeks (Orpheus).

II 1. d) Miscellaneous

One could now write a thick book about the most diverse symbols as well as their meaning and development, but this would go beyond the scope of the present book. Therefore, only a few of the better known symbols are listed below to illustrate the principle and variety of traditional symbols.

Ancestor statues are found in almost all cultures. They were originally a kind of secondary body for the dead, into which the dead could be called if one wished to speak with them. These statues have taken the place of the skulls of the dead.

The tombstone is a variant of the ancestor menhir. It is also quite widespread – especially in the area where the builders of the megalithic complexes once settled.

The cross is also a variant of the ancestor stone. Already in Göbekli Tepe there are representations of a man standing on top of a sweat lodge temple. This is the forerunner of the cross on Skull Mountain. The Vikings also erected a mound for their dead and placed a post or stone on top with an inscription for the dead.

The totem pole has been partially reinterpreted. Thus it became a symbol of the world tree (Germanic: Irminsul) or the symbol of a sunbeam (Egyptian: Obelisk) – both are symbols of the connection between heaven and earth, between gods and humans.
Such an Egyptian obelisk stands, among other things, in the middle of St. Peter's Square in Rome, that is, in the geographical center of Christianity. If you ever have the opportunity to look at this obelisk in Rome and feel its quality, you should not miss this opportunity. The power in this obelisk is really remarkable and especially the "pull upwards" in it – it acts like an umbilical cord between heaven and earth.
A similar central symbol is the Ka'aba in Mecca. Such central symbols exist especially in the monotheistic religions – two other examples are, for example, the Temple Mount in Jerusalem and the Golden Temple of the Sikhs in Amritsar.
By their very nature, such places are highly "charged."

A completely different symbol is the pointed hat. It came into use around 1500 B.C. at the latest in the megalithic culture in Western Europe and was also adopted by the

Germanic tribes and probably likewise by the Celts. These high hats, covered with gold foil, were probably worn by the sun priests of the time. They were, like the crowns of kings in Egypt, in medieval Europe, in Central America and in other cultures, and also the golden headbands of some Germanic princes, symbols of the connection to the sun god, that is, to the supreme deity.

These pointed hats are found in a simplified form without gold plating even 2000 years later among the Germanic gods. Presumably they are the bridge to the medieval idea that wizards wear high pointed hats – an idea that has been revived in more recent times by the "Harry Potter" books.

Votive images of all kinds are quite widespread. They are basically letters to the gods and to the ancestors and contain a request to them. These can be simply written notes in a saint's house, engraved tablets in a burial chamber or thin gold plates embossed with a picture, as the Germanic tribes placed them on the walls of their temples.

One can also count temple pictures, the Germanic temple shields with mythological scenes and even the cave paintings from the late Paleolithic Age to this subject area.

The lighting of a candle has a very similar function. Because fire destroys, i.e. "kills", fire has been understood since the Neolithic Age as a gateway to the otherworld. The lighting of a candle opens the gate to the other world, so that the gods and ancestors can listen to you.

The same symbolism is found in cremation, in the "eternal fires" in the temples of various peoples, the cult of the Indian firegod Agni, or in the enormous fire in the center of the temple where the mysteries of Eleusis were held.

A rather special symbol, only at first glance, is the wafer in the Eucharist (Lord's Supper). It represents Christ's body. This symbolism goes back to cannibalism, which was once widespread. Cannibalism was not at all for nourishment, but to preserve the strength and qualities of a particular dead person for the clan that ate him.

This custom is found, among others, among the ancient Egyptians ("Cannibalism Hymn" in the Pyramid Texts), among the Scythians (a people of the Indo-Europeans), in remnants among the Germanic tribes, among the Anasazi in North America, in Oceania, in China, etc. Ritual cannibalism can be traced back to the Paleolithic period – the earliest evidence is 800,000 years old.

The wafer that is used in the Eucharist is baked from flour, which at least in symbolic terms goes back to the fact that the god of the dead was once also the god of grain – hence the grain was the body of the god of the dead in North Africa, the Middle East, Western Europe, Asia and Central America. In our culture today, only the sceletal Reaper with his scythe remains of this (grain harvest = death).

11

There are also symbols like the <u>Vajra</u>, which have changed in the course of time. Originally, the vajra was the lightning bundle in the hand of the sky-god around 8500 BC in Mesopotamia, at the beginning of agriculture and animal husbandry.

This symbolism has been able to hold on for a long time and is found with different Mesopotamian sky gods, with the Greek Zeus, with the Indian Indra etc..

Already with the Indo-Europeans a symmetrical bundle was formed from the simple bundle, which consisted of four outer lightnings and a central lightning.

Since in the Neolithic Age meteorites were thought to be fallen parts of the sky and these meteorites consisted mainly of iron, the priestly staffs were forged of iron at that time – after all, they were supposed to bind their bearer to the sky. Also the crown and the throne of the pharaohs in the other world is according to the pyramid texts made of iron.

From this it follows that the Germanic seers carried iron seers' staffs, which consisted of four iron arches at the top, which met again at the top – iron lightning bundle staffs.

Among the Indians, this symbol evolved somewhat differently: the bundle remained – that is, a "handle" in the middle and four arcs each plus a central ray in the middle on both sides. The lightning bundle of Indra then gradually became the creation symbol of Buddhism.

As said – this list could be continued almost endlessly. The purpose of this section, however, is merely to show how widespread magical objects are in religion, cult and magic – and that it is important to know the history of these symbols as well.

II 1. e) Life Force Symbols

Finally, of special importance are the symbols of the life force, which are used in religious cult as well as in magic.

This is above all the <u>incense</u>, which was called by the Egyptians "se-netjer", i.e. "that which makes divine" – the burning of incense in front of a statue calls, according to the ideas of that time, the divinity or the soul of the deceased into this statue.

Today, the burning of incense is more commonly understood as "consecration." The incense commonly used by the Indians is tobacco, which is smoked. Here, the bowl of the pipe is the deity, the stem of the pipe is the tree of life, and the person smoking the pipe is the one who receives the blessing of the deity depicted on the bowl of the pipe via the stem.

A second life force symbolism is the <u>ritual potion</u>. Its symbolism is most likely much older than the incense symbolism, which is ultimately based on the idea of an afterlife gate made of fire – the burning of the incense is a mini-fire.

The ritual potion has originally been the mother's milk, which gives nourishment and security. This symbolism will be as old as the mammals. The milk has then become the ritual potion made of milk and honey, which has symbolized rebirth in the afterlife and therefore has been called by the Greeks "nectar ambrosia" and by the Indians "soma amrita", i.e. "honey-potion of immortality". Also the mead-god Kwasir of the Teutons and the mead-god Medigenus of the Celts has this symbolism and likewise the potion in the cult of the Egyptian goddess Hathor or the Balché potion of the Mayas. This potion is the milk of the mother goddess.

This is also the origin of the communion wine, the elixir of life of the alchemists and the magic potions of the magicians and witches.

II 1. f) Crop circles

There is another general symbolism whose origin is still unexplained: the crop circles. They could probably best be described as "collective telekinesis by which archetypes become visible".

In the crop circles many general structures and symbols can be found like parts of the cabbalistic tree of life, the threefold structure of the anthroposophists, the Mandelbrot set and the Julia set from the fractal theory and the like.

One could therefore also count the crop circles in a quite broad sense among the magic objects.

13

II 2.   Auxiliaries in Magic

Besides the traditional magical objects, there are also special objects that are used mainly in magic.

II 2. a)   Magic Wand

The most important is certainly the magic wand, whose history has already been presented.

II 2. b)   Robe, pointed hat etc.

In addition to the pointed hat, which has also been described above, there is also the wide robe of the magicians, which is known from the priests of the Celts (Druid) and the priests of the Germanic tribes (Diar, Gode) and which, together with the pointed hat, shaped the medieval image of the magician.

Less known are the ring, the gloves and the belt, which were the three insignia of a Germanic priest.

II 2. c)   Temple

First of all, a magician does not need a temple. This only becomes necessary for certain group rituals from the sweat lodge to the lodge meeting – one needs a place to gather.

It is obvious that a magical quality is then ascribed to this place itself or that one takes care that it receives such a quality.

II 2. d)   Statues

Statues are not necessarily used in magic, but they do occur. This depends to a great extent on the magical style of the magician or witch in question.

II 2. e)   Talismans etc.

Besides the objects like temples and statues, which are more or less understandable to every observer even without special explanation, there are also the individual magical objects, which often have a very special function like talismans, amulets, crystals and the like.

There are also collections of magically significant objects such as the collections of meteorites of the Paleolithic people, the medicine bags of the Indians, the small statuettes of the gods of the Germanic tribes, which have been carried in a leather bag on a cord around the neck, the pictures of saints in the car or on the house altar (often Mary, Christ, St. Christopher), etc.
These collections of small magical objects are, so to speak, "miniature temples" that one can carry in one's pocket.

II 2. f)   Technical aids

Finally, various "technical aids" are used in magic, which include the magic mirror, the crystal ball, the Quija board, the Tarot cards, the yarrow stalks of the I Ching, and the like.
In some cases, these objects are considered consecrated, such as the mirror and the crystal ball – in other cases, they are simply considered as tools, such as the Tarot cards.

II 2. g)   Skulls etc.

In magic, of course, all traditional religious objects can be used, such as the skulls already described.

III Personal Preferences

In addition to the magical-mythological-religious tradition of symbols, there is also the individual imprint – just as in all other fields, these individual qualities and preferences also exist in magic.

III 1. Horoscope

The most formative is first of all one's own horoscope – and the horoscope also shows what relationship one has to magical objects.

First of all, three questions are important for this topic: Where is the Sun? Where is the Ascendant? And what is in the 2nd house?

The Sun sign shows what one generally strives for – Capricorn strives for a solid form, Taurus for a protected area … both are approaches that make one inclined to tie magic into objects.

A Taurus Ascendant, on the other hand, shows that one generally thinks in object terms. For someone with a Pisces Ascendant, on the other hand, everything is in flux and therefore not very representational. For a magician with an Aquarius Ascendant, on the other hand, what counts most is knowledge and the world formula and thus the magic words.

Finally, the planets in the 2nd house show quite concretely how to deal with substance. If there is a Saturn/Neptune conjunction there, the person concerned will certainly want to fix the magical powers (Neptune) into the traditionally (Saturn) intended objects (2nd house).

If someone has Saturn in the 2nd house, but Saturn has a square to Pluto, the person will not be able or willing (square) to give solid form (Saturn) to anything essential (Pluto).

Because of the complexity of astrology, one could effortlessly write a separate book just about this aspect of magical objects. However, the important point above all is that everyone has a different preference for dealing with magical objects because of their horoscope. This own inclination should be known and taken into account in magic if one wants to be successful.

It always diminishes one's own power if one acts against one's own inclination and not in one's own style – which is not only true for magic …

III 2.   One's own experiences

The second form of individual imprinting originates from one's own experiences. What one has experienced, one has recognized as real and therefore takes it into account in all later deeds. Therefore, if one has experienced the great power of magical objects, one will either want to use them oneself or at least take their existence into account in what one does.

III 3.   Community

If one is active as a magician not alone, but in a community, it is usually helpful to have an external framework to orient oneself by.

This includes a meeting place, which can be a clearing or a temple and many other locations, then possibly statues of gods, further on various symbols and finally a reference system such as the Kabbalistic Tree of Life, from which in turn various symbols arise, which can also be represented materially and have magical properties.

IV Production and Consecration

The basic question now is, of course, where to find objects with magical properties or how to confer magical properties to an object. Furthermore, it would be interesting to know which magical properties of an object actually exist and what they can be used for.

IV 1. The magical quality

An object has magical properties if it has been "consecrated". This is usually considered to be "filled with life force". One can understand this life force as an amorphous substance, i.e. as a "force" or also as a connection to an ancestor spirit, to a planet or to a deity. One can also regard this consecration simply as an "association to images in one's own psyche".

In the end, these different images do not make much difference. Ancestor spirits and deities are forms in the life force – and the psyche is the personal part of the general life force. Consequently, an object has magical properties if it is associated with much life force.

In this context, the question naturally arises as to what life force actually is. In essence, life force is the interface between consciousness and matter. It is the adhesive surface between the two, the transition between the consciousness-inside of the world and the matter-outside of the world.

The life force has no substance in itself – it is simply what you see when you look at matter directly from consciousness without the aid of the physical sense organs. It is the "telepathic view" of the world.

Therefore one can formulate the question about the life force, which is in an object, also differently: With which form of consciousness is an object connected on its inside?

A living being is particularly "magically charged" because it is firmly connected with a soul and thus with a large measure of consciousness – after the death of this living being, its body is no longer magical because the soul has left it.

Similarly, any object can be connected with a "soul", i.e. with a consciousness, which then gives this object magical properties, i.e. the ability to act out of itself within a more or less limited framework. Thus, one could say that a magical object is a living object.

The character of this magic object then results from which archetype this object has been connected with. It does not matter whether this connection has been regarded as the life force, as a spirit, as a deity, as an image in one's own psyche, i.e. abstract information, or as something else at the time of consecration of the object.

Therefore, the strength of the magical properties of an object depends on the extent to which one has succeeded in making the object a "living being."

The description of magical objects just given assumes two things:

1. All things have a matter-outside and a consciousness-inside.

2. The consciousness-inside of every object or being can be changed.

This worldview, in which all things have consciousness, is obviously a variant of the pantheistic worldview. This conception of magical objects and its underlying worldview is confirmed by two things:

1. Consciousness can directly, that is without the physical senses, perceive another consciousness and any objects: Telepathy.

2. Consciousness can influence directly, thus without the physical body, another consciousness and any objects: Telekinesis (or in case of influencing a consciousness telepathic hypnosis).

These two interactions can be possible only if all things have a consciousness: Always only like acts on like. This principle, which is mainly known from homeopathy, is also an element of the whole of physics:

- Only things which have a mass can influence each other by collisions.

- Only things which have an electric charge can move each other – things without electric charge are not influenced by the electric charge of other things.

- Only things that have a color charge (strong interaction in the nucleus) can move each other – things without a color charge are not affected by the color charge of other things.

The model of the world in which all things also have a consciousness side puts both telepathy and telekinesis in a larger context and can also describe the nature of magical objects. Therefore, this model is quite useful … that is, "correct" in the sense of the everyday use of that word.

IV 2. The frame of reference

The making and consecration of an object into a magical object, i.e. into a "living object", stands only in the rarest of cases in isolation, but usually has a frame of reference.

This is often a particular religion, as in the consecration of a host for the Eucharist. However, the frame of reference can also be a mythology or cult, which is ultimately not too different from a religion. It can also be a more abstract system such as the astrological planets, the four elements, the Tarot cards, the I Ching, and the like.

Finally, the frame of reference is always shaped by the personal experiences of the magician.

This frame of reference contains the units of consciousness with which an object can be associated by the person concerned during a consecration – i.e. deities, ancestors, planets, principles, etc. By the consecration, an object becomes a body of the consciousness unit in question.

So a consecration is an expansion of consciousness – the consciousness of the magician or the consciousness of a deity.

IV 3. The Procedure

The possible procedures for the consecration of an object that is to receive magical properties look very diverse at first glance. However, a closer look reveals a uniform basic structure.

IV 3. a) The Resolution

As a rule, the making of a magical object begins with a decision – the spontaneous version is extremely rare, even though it is not impossible.

For the further course of the consecration the motivation is the essential thing: Why does one want to consecrate an object? How do you want to do it? And why does one want to use a magical object to achieve the actual goal? Is making a magical object the most direct and effective way to one's goal?

The more clarity and expertise there is in these questions, the greater the chance that the magician or witch with their approach will also arrive where he or she wants to go.

Therefore, it makes sense to take enough time to look at one's own plan in detail and to examine it from all sides as well as to compare it with other possible approaches.

IV 3. b) The choice of the frame of reference

In most cases, the choice of the frame of reference is self-evident: it will be either the worldview preferred by the magician or the worldview of the group that wants to perform the upcoming consecration together.

The symbolism used can be very simple and refer e.g. only to a planet or to an element or a Tarot card or it can be a whole mythology which is used as a background.

The complexity of the symbolism used does not guarantee an effective consecration – even a very simple ritual can be very effective. However, if one is at home in a certain mythology, the reference of a consecration to that mythology is, of course, a very strong backing and a great "source of power."

IV 3. c) The vivid imagination

The most vivid and lively imagination possible is generally known as the basic element of every magical action. This also applies to the consecration of an object. Through imagination one gets in touch with the life force. One can also say that the inner, imagined picture establishes contact with the life force, i.e. touches the interface between consciousness and matter – and can then achieve a magical effect there.

IV 3. d) The one-directed concentration

Imagination is the hand that grasps that which is to be magically changed – concentration is the force in the arm muscle that then moves that which is grasped to another place. Ideally, this concentration is one-pointed without any inner contradictions and doubts.

The meanwhile quite well-known caricature of the not quite perfect unified concentration is the following quotation from an English magic instruction: "This is my magic wand – I hope it works."

The single-mindedness of concentration is like a laser beam in which all the light rays have the same strength, frequency and direction, and therefore have such amazing qualities. Just as these qualities of a laser beam depend on the way it is generated, the one-pointedness of concentration depends primarily on the motivation for the action in question. The clearer and more unambiguous the motivation is, the greater and more consistent is the concentration that results from it.

It is always beneficial to examine one's motivation before embarking on a major magical endeavor.

A great motivation does not necessarily have to have a long lead-up – it can also become apparent spontaneously and then be carried out.

Sometimes, with sufficient concentration and vivid imagination, it can happen that one suddenly enters another state of consciousness or temporarily "blacks out" during the ritual. This is not at all tragic – when you suddenly realize again where you actually are and what you wanted to do, you continue at the last point of the ritual that you can still remember.

However, this temporary "black-out" due to the intensity of the ritual is not a very common phenomenon.

IV 3. e)   The Ritual

The use of gestures, words, clothing, candles, and other objects, as well as the design of a comprehensive and coherent dramaturgy, aid both imagination and concentration. By these tools, a ritual is created, that is, an external representation of the inner processes.

Since in a consecration the object in question on the outside is to be connected with an inner consciousness, the external representation of this consciousness (e.g. the planet Mars or the god Pan) is extremely helpful.

The components of the ritual and the structure of the ritual are determined by the type of consecration one is seeking.

IV 3. f)   The Invocation

An invocation is the calling upon a deity and identification with it. An invocation is therefore, so to speak, a self consecration.

Since contact with a deity is established through an invocation, the invocation is the obvious basis for associating an object with a deity. If one wants to connect an object with a deity, one must first establish contact with both the object and the deity …

The same is true, of course, for planetary qualities or elemental qualities that one wants to use in a consecration.

In some cases, one can also build up this invocation in stages, by invoking successively an element, a planet and finally a deity:

Structure of a Consecration			
Theme	*1ˢᵗ step: Element*	*2ⁿᵈ step: Planet*	*3ʳᵈ step: Deity*
Self-centering	Light	Sun	Osiris
Power	Fire	Mars	Thor
Love	Water	Venus	Aphrodite
Knowledge	Air	Mercury	Thot
Thriving	Earth	Jupiter	Ptah

By this procedure one can gradually build up an increasing tension and fullness of power, i.e. life force.

IV 3. g)   The Ritual Participants

Finally, there are the ritual participants. If one performs a ritual alone, it is quite simple: one does everything oneself.

When the ritual is performed by a group, however, there are a variety of possibilities, depending on the motivation and experience of the individual group members:

1. The magician/priest performs the ritual and the others join in.

2. The magician/priest performs the ritual and the others help with their concentration and imagination.

3. The magician/priest performs the ritual, and in between there are joint actions such as chanting given texts or songs.

4. The magician/priest performs the ritual, but delegates individual tasks to other participants.

5. The participants receive different roles in the ritual, which can consist e.g. of the deities at the Egyptian afterlife court, the twelve gods on the Olymp, the eight central deities of the West African Ifa oracle etc.. By such a distribution of roles, a whole mythe (Egyptian afterlife court), a whole mythology (gods of Olympus) or a whole system (Ifa oracle) is invoked collectively, so to speak. Of course, if this is done with sufficient concentration,

it can be extremely effective. Most mystery plays are based on this principle.

6. There are also other variations, such as the ritual dance, in which the community stands in a circle and claps or dances, forming the foundation and framework. The individual participants then step into the center one after the other and dance there, thereby calling in the blessings of their ancestors, for example.

There are hardly any limits to creativity in group rituals …

IV 4.   Concrete Examples

The previous, general considerations about the consecration of objects, by which they may become magical objects, will be described in more detail in the following by means of a number of examples.

This is, of course, again only a small selection of possible consecration rituals. However, since they are all based on the same basic principles, the general procedure for making a magical object can be seen from this small selection.

IV 4. a)   The Grain Mummy

The Egyptian grain mummy has a very long tradition and goes back at least 4,000 years – but possibly much further back in time to almost 8500 B.C. to the beginning of grain cultivation.

This magical object and the associated ritual are very simple: About two weeks before the festival of the rebirth of Osiris, who is the god of grain and the god of the dead, a figure of Osiris is formed as a mummy from a mixture of clay and grain, usually 30-50cm long. It is sometimes wrapped in mummy bandages and occasionally receives a death mask made of beeswax (corresponding to the gold mask of Tutankh-amen). This reclining Osiris statuette is then kept moist, causing the grain in the mummy to sprout – the grain god Osiris has been reborn.

This ritual, which originally served to summon a good harvest, was also associated with one's own rebirth in the afterlife – after all, Osiris is both the god of the rebirth of grain after the Nile floods and the god of the rebirth of the souls in the afterlife after human death.

This ritual can of course be extended to other things such as healing from a disease. Depending on the use of this ritual, one can also include other deities from this mythe such as Isis, Nephthys, Seth, Thoth and Anubis.

The grain mummy does not require any special consecration, since it is the image of a deity and consequently associated with that deity. Moreover, a fundamental process from the mythology of this deity is represented very directly: the sowing and germination of the grain.

Here the consecration consists of an action – there may be an imagination and a concentration involved, but it is not the foundation of this consecration. The foundation is simply the image of the deity and the long tradition of this ritual. Both the image and the tradition form a resonating body, so to speak, which begins to sound as soon as one beginns to form a grain mummy of Osiris.

Another aspect is the high motivation that arises from the farmers' desire for a good harvest – which is constantly grounded (in both senses of the word) by the daily work in the fields.

IV 4. b)   The mouth opening ritual

This is another ancient Egyptian ritual that is the centerpiece of the burial ritual. This ritual also has a very long tradition, dating back in part to the early Neolithic period.

It consists of three elements that have been combined together to form a complex ritual:

> 1. The shaman-priest ("sem-priest") travels to the otherworld, searches there for the soul of the deceased and brings it back to this world to his descendants, so that this soul can continue to protect its descendants with advice and action.

> 2. The Anubis priest, who performs the burials, opens the mouth of the mummy of the dead, which symbolically makes him breathe again and brings him back to life – by which the further life in the hereafter is meant.

> 3. The stonemason who made the statue of the dead for his mortuary temple, at the very end shapes the mouth of the statue and thus opens its mouth so that it can breathe.

These three symbolisms add up to the idea that the soul of the dead is brought back from the otherworld to this world by the shaman and is inserted into the statue of the dead after the Anubis priest has opened the mouth of the mummy and the sculptor has opened the mouth of the statue. From that moment, the statue has become a second body of the dead person's soul – the statue is now an "inhabited statue".

This principle of the "inhabited statue" is found in almost all cultures: the statues themselves were not conceived as a deity, but only as a body that the deity can inhabit. In India there are even different terms for "statue of the god before consecration" and "statue of the god after consecration".

This invocation of the soul of a dead person or deity into its statue is basically an invocation that takes place not into one's own body, but into a statue. It can also be regarded as an evocation.

In most cases, this consecration is again achieved not by intense imagination and concentration, but by a traditional procedure such as the ancient Egyptian mouth-opening ritual.

IV 4. c)   The Eucharist

In the Eucharist there are two magical objects – or consecrated objects, as one would probably rather say from a Christian point of view. These are the wafer (originally a piece of bread), which represents the body of Christ, and the wine, which represents the blood of Christ.

Here bread and wine are identified with a deity (Christ) – the difference to the identification of the grain mummy with Osiris is not particularly great … The wafer or the bread corresponds to the grain of Osiris and the wine to the milk of the goddess Isis, who gives birth again to Osiris after his death.

In Christian terminology, the transformation of the ordinary bread and wine by consecration into Christ's body and blood is called a "real consummation" – this consecration is thus conceived not as a symbolic process, but as a real one.

By eating the consecrated bread and drinking the consecrated wine, the ritual participant thus takes Christ's body into himself. This may sound rather barbaric today, but since in Christ's time cannibalism as the possibility of the absorption of the life force of a deceased person by his descendants was still generally known and common in many places – it has been a generally understood image for the people of that time.

Thus, the Eucharist is also the invocation of a deity with the help of a symbolic action and with the help of two magical objects. This principle can be found very often in religion and partly also in magic. As a rule, the consecrations, which have a very long tradition, are also quite effective.

IV 4. d)   A temple consecration

The consecration of a temple depends on the worldview and the intended use of the temple. However, there are also some elements independent of tradition.

The first question is what is meant by the temple: For the Amerindians and the early Neolithic people in Göbekli Tepe, the sweat lodge is the belly of the Mother Goddess, for the Egyptians it was the primordial mound, for the Christians it is a meeting place, for the Buddhists it is a mandala, i.e. an image of the world …

Thus, there are different focuses: The people of Göbekli Tepe designed their temples as a mother's belly with a child in it, the Egyptians painted the plants on the primordial mound on the bases of the walls and columns, the Christians filled the churches with pews and with statues of saints, the Buddhists designed concentric-symmetrical structures …

Also the rituals in the temples were accordingly different: In Göbekli Tepe the clan gathered, in Egypt the priest nourished the deity, with the Christians the priest connects the people with God, the Buddhists perform meditations and rituals …

The temple is the most important everyday place in a religious world view. It is designed according to the worldview in question – as a rule, each part of the temple corresponds to one aspect of the worldview. Already by this equation a consecration arises – each part of the temple is connected with a deity: with an Egyptian temple the ground with the earth god Geb, the columns with the air god Shu, the ceiling with the sky goddess Nut, the temple court with the primeval water Nun, the two temple towers at the entrance with the two Ru lions at the horizon etc.. In this way, the temple becomes an embodiment of mythology, an image of the world and the gods in it.

The essence of the temple is usually the statues whose house is the temple. Therefore, the main element of the consecration of a temple is the invocation of the deities into the statue of the central deity and into the statues of the accompanying deities.

In St. Peter's Square in Rome, this has been arranged very vividly: Christ's cross is at the top of the obelisk in the center, the twelve apostles are at the top of the front of St. Peter's, which makes up a quarter of the square, and a large number of the saints are on the two quarter-circle porticoes to its left and to its right.

There may also be a more technical part of the temple consecration, consisting of the purification of the temple with fire and water, and a general invocation of life-force or, more differentially, the four elements, but the central part of the temple consecration is the consecration of the statues – the invocation of the deities for whom the temple was built.

IV 4. e)   The sweat lodge

When a sweat lodge is built, a strange phenomenon can be observed: As soon as the hut itself is built and the fire is lit, the atmosphere changes and becomes "holy." You don't need to do anything for this – the ritual begins with the lighting of the fire and you can feel and inwardly see how the various spirits associated with the sweat lodge (Snake, Bear, Eagle, Buffalo Woman, Earth Mother, Heavenly Father, Great Mystery) come to the sweat lodge. Therefore, there is no need to summon these beings afterwards in the sweat lodge – you can simply greet them and thank them for coming.

This ritual is so ancient that from the moment the fire is lit, it begins to run by itself, and without doing anything, the sweat lodge turns into the womb of the Mother Goddess.

One also incenses the hut with sage, but this is only a reinforcement of the transformation of the hut into the mother's belly, which has already begun, and a greeting of the spirits that have already come.

Thus, there is no real consecration of a sweat lodge …

IV 4. f)   The statue of Horus

In the villages of ancient Egypt, there has been a staute of Horus in most village squares. This statue of Horus stood with one foot on a snake and the other foot on a scorpion – sometimes there has been also a crocodile.

When someone was bitten by a scorpion or a snake, they hurried to this statue of Horus, doused it with water and caught this water in a second vessel with the help of the drainage channel below the statue. This water was then given to the bitten person to drink so that the poison could not harm him.

This ritual referred to Isis curing her son Horus from the poison of snakes and scorpions. Since Horus resided in each statue dedicated to him, the person bitten connected with Horus by drinking the water of the statue and, like him, was healed by Isis.

Primarily the statue is consecrated and secondarily also the water, which was poured over it. It becomes therefore "holy water".

In the same way, among many peoples including the medieval Christians, water was consecrated by drinking it from the skulls of a saint. Since the saints were responsible for curing various diseases and solving various problems, one knew which church to make a pilgrimage to in order to drink from the skull of the saint in question.

This is, among other things, a precursor of today's homeopathy …

IV 4. g)   The magic wand

The magic wand is a symbol with a great prehistory: bird wand, totem pole, menhir, temple pillar, ancestor stone, world tree, umbilical cord to heaven, sushumna (yoga), seer wand, priest wand, king scepter, bishop wand, etc.. Therefore also the magic wand is already consecrated due to its history, i.e. connected with a certain symbolism.

About 50-100 years ago, it was common practice to hollow out magic wands and fill them with a "magic substance". This principle has recently become more popular again due to the "Harry Potter" books. However, this is not a traditional process, but an attempt to create a magical object in a technical way.

Today, however, wands are only rarely used in magic.

IV 4. h) A Planetary Talisman

A talisman is used to perform a very specific task: healing from a disease, bringing about a relationship, creating wealth, etc. A common method is the consecration with an element and a planet, that is, the connection of the talisman with a suitable element and planet.

To do this, first a shape is chosen for the talisman – usually it is derived from the planet used:

- Saturn	- Triangle
- Jupiter	- Square
- Mars	- Pentagon
- Sun	- Hexagon
- Venus	- Hepotagon
- Mercury	- Octagon
- Moon	- Nonagon

This basic shape is then made either from the metal in question or from another material painted with the color in question:

- Saturn	- lead	- black
- Jupiter	- tin	- blue
- Mars	- iron	- red
- Sun	- gold	- yellow
- Venus	- copper	- green
- Mercury	- brass	- orange
- Moon	- silver	- violet

In addition, there is a whole series of traditional number squares, seals, symbols, names, etc. ... a complex system with many details.

On this talisman is usually also engraved, written or painted in some way the actual wish (health, relationship, wealth, etc.).

Finally, a suitable month and day is chosen:

- Saturn	- Sun in Capricorn/Aquarius	- Saturday
- Jupiter	- Sun in Sagittarius/Pisces	- Thursday
- Mars	- Sun in Aries/Scorpio	- Tuesday
- Sun	- Sun in Leo	- Sunday
- Venus	- Sun in Taurus/Libra	- Friday
- Mercury	- Sun in Gemini/Virgo	- Wednesday
- Moon	- Sun in Cancer	- Monday

You may also choose a suitable location, number of participants, color of clothing for the ritual, etc:

- Saturn	- mountain	- 3 participants in black
- Jupiter	- shop/office	- 4 participants in blue
- Mars	- armory/sports field	- 5 participants in red
- Sun	- temple/palace	- 6 participants in yellow
- Venus	- clearing/garden	- 7 participants in green
- Mercury	- library	- 8 participants in orange
- Moon	- bedroom	- 9 participants in violet

Here, the systematic structuring of the talisman and the ritual results in a high density of symbols and thus a high level of concentration as well as an impressive visual experience.

The core of the ritual is probably the invocation of a god that fits the chosen planet. If one has a soft spot for the gods of Olympus or the gods in Asgard, these would be:

- Saturn	- Kronos	- Thiazi (Tyr as a giant)
- Jupiter	- Zeus	- Freyr
- Mars	- Ares	- Thor
- Sun	- Helios	- Tyr (as the sungod)
- Venus	- Aphrodite	- Freya
- Mercury	- Hermes	- Hönir or Loki
- Moon	- Selene	- Mani

The actual ritual consists of enumerating the individual aspects of the talisman and the ritual (form, substance, color, seal, place, clothing, etc.) one after the other in the ritual text, imagining them with as much concentration as possible. Thereby always also the sentence, which describes the actual request, is pronounced. Finally, the deity is invoked and asked for help – possibly one imagines that, for example, a red ray of light coming down from Mars and filling the talisman. From this time on the talisman is connected to Mars as with an umbilical cord.

IV 4. i) The Cult

The cult is a special, but at the same time very ancient and effective method by which an normal object may turn into a magical object.

In the cult, a religiously significant action, that is, a ritual, is often repeated over many centuries or millennia. This creates a strongly imprinted image on the conscious side of the world: an archetype in the collective subconsciousness of the people.

As soon as one begins to perform the ritual in question, one makes contact with this image. If an object such as a temple, a statue, a chalice or something similar is connected with this ritual, this object is connected with this archetype, with this mythe and with the deities in this mythe. The oldest variant of this form of consecration is the sweat lodge.

The same principle of "effect by repetition" is found in meditation – especially in meditations with a mantra.

IV 4. j) Charging by time

To the "effect by repetition" from the cult there is also an unconscious and sometimes also unintentional variant: the "imprinting by circumstances constant for a long time".

This imprinting of an object can arise quite simply by the fact that someone possesses an object for a long time and possibly even carries it on his own body, as for example, a ring. In such a case the object can take over the quality of its wearer.

Such an imprint can also result from a place being used for the same purpose for a long time, like a temple or a statue.

Likewise, things and places can be imprinted by violent events such as battlefields, dungeons, or a concentration camp.

Also, some ancient objects such as seers' rods from tombs, the miter of a bishop, or a consecrated Amerindian pipe can acquire qualities beyond the mere substance of the object.

IV 4. k)   The Spiritus familiaris

The spiritus familiaris, sometimes called the "house spirit" (instead of the "family spirit"), is an artificially produced spirit. It is, so to speak, the "light" version of a golem. The inspiration for it or the archetype for it is the creation of the first man from clay.

From a purely magical point of view, a Spiritus familiaris is very similar to a talisman, although there are some differences.

To manufacture such a spirit, one proceeds as follows:

- You decide what you want to use the spirit for: as a guardian, as a messenger, as a warrior, as a procurer of love adventures, as a treasure hunter etc..
- Then you choose a suitable shape for the ghost: a dog as a guard, a bird as a messenger, an Amazon as a warrior, Pan as a love adventure promoter, a wolf as a treasure hunter, etc.
- Next, obtain yellow clay as well as beeswax. Two parts wet clay together with one part beeswax are beoing molten in a pot at a full moon. Then both are thoroughly mixed. Finally, the clay/wax mixture is used to form the selected figure.
- A decoction is made from chamomile flowers (thick, strong tea), to which a little "Aurum chloratum C200" (a homeopathic tincture of gold) is added at the end.
- A tube-shaped hole is drilled into the underside of the figure, which has not yet cooled down and is therefore still soft, using one's finger, a stick or similar. The chamomile/gold tincture is poured into this hole as well as a few drops of the magiciens own blood. Then you close this hole with a plug made of the clay/wax mixture.
- Then the figure is allowed to dry completely and cool. It will then feel organic like skin or bone. It is at the same time very hard and very elastic.
- Next, the figure, i.e. the spirit within it, is given a name that fits its intended purpose.
- For the consecration one holds the figure in the left hand and holds the right hand over it and imagines that from the right hand successively the elements earth, water, air, fire and light flow into the figure (a left-handed person holds the figure in his right hand).
- Depending on the character of the figure, one can also charge it with sunlight, moonlight, wind, and the like. You can also ask one of the planets or a deity to strengthen the spirit in the figure. There are no limits to the imagination here. Menstrual blood and semen have also been successfully used to strengthen such a spirit.

- After a while you can feel that the figure begins to "come alive": It seems to get hot or pulsate when you hold it in your hand; possibly it also appears in your own dreams or on dream journeys or you feel called by it.

- Now you can give it tasks by addressing the spirit in the figure by the name you have given it and telling it what to do.

This ghost has obviously been made completely artificially. Sometimes this type of spirit is called a "psychogone."

The "recipe" just given contains only Sun ingredients. For example, if you want to make a spirit with lunar properties, you can use white clay, stearin, poppies and Argentum C200. Accordingly, one can vary the ingredients for other planets as well.

Concerning this method of making a magically effective object, the instructions in the still following chapter "Risks and Side Effects" are extremely important.

The principle of "body and filling" applied to the Spiritus familiaris (clay/wax figure with a tincture in it) corresponds to the manufacturing method of magic wands, in which a wooden tube is filled with a magic substance.

The archetype of this type of magic procedure is of course the body and the soul within it.

IV 4. l) Magic rings

One can "consecrate" and "charge with life force" objects in many ways. The chosen method also depends on the object one wants to create or consecrate. The most important point is to choose the right symbolism, because it will always prevail in the end – no matter what one has intended.

However, when I once made magic rings almost 40 years ago, I had little overview of myths and symbols, nor did I realize the importance of such knowledge.

I myself forged rings at the time of the dying of the forest around 1985, which I wanted to bury at various places of power in Germany to cause a kind of "acupuncture of the earth" to strengthen the forest so that it could withstand the acid rain.

- Snakes seemed most appropriate to me as symbols of power. The shape of snake rings seemed to me to best represent the concentration and protection provided by the snakes.

- Twelve snakes as an analogy to the zodiac plus one snake in the centre, which corresponds to the sun, seemed to me to be the appropriate number.

- As a central location in Germany, the Vogelsberg north of Frankfurt semmed to me to fit well: it was roughly in the center of Germany and it is the largest (extinct) volcano in Germany – this would give the project additional power.

- As a material, silver seemed most appropriate: silver corresponds to the moon and thus to the life force – and I was concerned with directing the life force in the earth and in the trees.

- The snakes needed a clear intention, thus an emphasis of their Third Eye. Therefore, I chose twelve tourmalines (thriving) and one ruby (power) to place on the heads of the snakes.

- Since the snakes were meant to transform something, I only forged them on a full moon.

- In order for these rings to be closely connected, I made them parallel: On the first full moon I sawed them all out of a silver sheet, on the second full moon I bent them all round and welded them together to form a ring, on the third full moon I filed the rough shape, and so on.

- Since they were to come to life, a manufacturing period of nine months analogous to pregnancy in a human being seemed reasonable to me.

- This symbolism could be strengthened by the fact that I put the "procreation", thus the beginning of the forging on spring beginning, whereby the "birth", thus the completion of the rings (nine months later) fell on Christmas, which is the birth festival of the sun (and later of Christ).

- To these serpent rings I have written a longer poem, in which I have described and invoked them – that has turned out quite powerfully. I then often spoke this "dragon song" to myself while forging.

- During the forging I called up the snakes and dragons from the earth again and again.

By this very dense symbolism, by the constant imagination as well as by the high concentration, these rings have become very powerful. However, due to several mistakes, they have received a different character than it was intended.

Also concerning the production of these snake rings it is advisable to read carefully the instructions in the chapter "Risks and Side Effects" later in this book.

IV 4. m)   Orgone Accumulator

There are various instructions for apparatuses which, from their construction, conduct the life force. The best known of them is certainly the orgone accumulator, which was developed by Wilhelm Reich, a student of Sigmund Freud. It consists essentially of a box that has been constructed of alternating layers of metal and wood. "Orgone" is Reich's term for the life force.

With the help of such apparatuses, Wilhelm Reich is said to have succeeded in curing diseases and even influencing the weather.

However, I myself do not have enough experience with these apparatuses to be able to say for sure whether and how they work.

IV 4. n)   Pyramid

A similar method is to place things under a pyramid made of sheet copper or, if necessary, cardboard. Things placed under the pyramid behave differently from things placed next to it in a normal cardboard box. The easiest way to check this is with perishable foods such as two tomatoes.

My own experiments have shown that both tomatoes develop very differently – they rot at different times and they also taste very differently. However, in my experiments, the pyramid did not always do better than the simple cardboard box.

In my opinion, more systematic research is needed here to arrive at truly reliable conclusions.

IV 4. o)   Feng-Shui

The Chinese have thoroughly researched the effect of forms and compositions of things over a long period of time and described their experiences in Feng-Shui. The resulting knowledge is very complex – its detailed exposition is beyond the scope of this book.

The basic principles of Feng Shui can be briefly summarized as follows:

    - Shapes direct the life force. Therefore, straight lines give rise to hard rays; arcs, on the other hand, give rise to soft vortices. This is why, for example, the roof edges of ancient Chinese buildings are curved upwards at the end.

- Materials influence the quality of the life force in a place. Therefore, the choice of appropriate materials for the various parts of a house shapes the quality of that building.

- The composition of materials results in a "chord" of qualities.

- The cardinal points have certain qualities that should be taken into account.

- Every thing has a natural internal structure, which can be represented as an area of three by three squares. This structure is called "Ba-Gua" in China and "Purusha" in India. When constructing buildings, parks, cities and the like, this structure should be taken into account.

- The elements of nature such as plains, mountains, valleys, rivers, lakes, forests, seashores, etc. all have certain qualities. Their interplay results in life force patterns, which give rise to "ley-lines" and places of power. Ley-lines are lines in the earth along which life force flows – they correspond to the acupuncture meridians in the human body. Power places correspond to acupuncture points and chakras in the body. Important buildings should be constructed at such power places.

In addition to taking into account these formally detectable structures in the life force, Feng Shui also has other non-intellectual methods for detecting the flow of the life force.

The most important traditional method is "riding the dragon". In this method, one first selects the approximate location where, for example, a building is to be erected. Then one runs into the circle one after the other from about a dozen places on the edge of this area without controlling where one runs. These running paths are marked and at the end the net of the run paths is considered. Since in intuitive running ("riding") one follows the flow of life force ("dragon"), in this way one can recognize the life force patterns in the place concerned and see where the most powerful place is.

Another method is "energetic Feng Shui", which also takes care of the material conditions, but builds up a life force image of the desired condition in the place mainly by concentrated imagination. There are some useful methods for this:

- One asks a deity for help in what one is doing: the transmutation god Shiva, the fire god Agni, the earth god Geb, etc.

- One can imagine the desired ideal image in that place with many details.

- Each detail of the imagined image is grounded with an action. This can be burning a match (fire as a helper), putting a coin on the ground (metal as a helper), spraying water (water as a helper), etc. Personally, I also find the rose massage oil from Weleda very helpful to harmonize places (Venus as a helper) – to do this, you dab some of the oil on the place in question. Sometimes you can also use homeopathic remedies – e.g. Lycopodium C200 to neutralize the radiance of an oil tank in a cellar (oil originates from Lycopodium plants).

- One can place appropriate things in places to call certain qualities to them.

- One can make life force connections to trees, streams, rocks and the like near the place whose life force form one is shaping. This calls the quality of these things to that place or to a particular spot in that place.

- With all the forces that one calls, one should always contact the soul of, for example, with the tree the Elf of that tree, with the fire efor example the fire god Agni, with a certain rock the earth god Geb, and so on.

- In the same way, it is important to relate everything one does to the soul of the client. If the life force design of the place corresponds to the intention of the owner of that place, the design obtains stability by this connection. Without this connection, the life-force design would dissolve after a short time. This connection to a being on the consciousness side of the world is always the essential point in the production of magic objects (here the magic imprinting of a place).

- Finally, at the end of such a life force imprinting of a place, it makes sense to establish a connection from the consecrated place to the root chakra of the earth, that is, to its glowing iron/nickel core. This connection is usually a ray of white or red light. By this connection the place receives a "high voltage currant", by which everything, which one "installed" at the place, receives a much greater strength than before.

All these methods, of course, can be applied to the "charging" of magical objects.

The effect of Feng Shui, orgone accumulators and also symbols is not based on any human activity like a consecration, but simply on the form and material of the object.

IV 4. p) Places of power

There are places in nature where a lot of life force has naturally accumulated. These can be lakes (gathering, stillness), streams (movement, loosening), mountains (solidity), volcanoes (fire, transformation), valleys (gathering, joining), etc.

The special quality of a place can be recognized in broad outlines by observing the place, but for grasping the subtleties, sensing, telepathy, dream journeys, etc. are recommended.

You may find a detailed description of the quality of places, objects, forms, angles and so on in my books "Feng Shui for Beginners" and "Crop Circles for Beginners".

IV 4. q) Voodoo dolls

Voodoo dolls are one of the more famous magical objects. These are dolls that can be made of various materials and has the appearance of a concrete person. Usually, there is also a hair or something similar of the person in question in this doll.

This doll is made with the firm intention and vivid imagination that everything that happens to the doll will also happen to the person represented by the doll – which works well.

This method has become known through its use in voodoo, but it was also used in the Germanic Nid magic and also in ancient Egypt – among others by a Sachmet priest who wanted to kill and depose the Pharaoh Ramses III (the court notes have been preserved).

In this form of magic, the doll becomes, so to speak, a second body of the person who is attacked with this method. The statues of the dead, to which one brings offerings, so that the dead one does not have to starve in the hereafter, are also such "secondary bodies". What one does with the statue, happens also with the represented human being – no matter whether he is still alive or already dead.

The statues of the gods are rather dwelling places than secondary bodies for the gods, because the gods have no physical body.

The already described Horus statue is also technically a voodoo doll – even if it is used for healing purposes.

IV 4. r) Sacrifice and human sacrifice

A very archaic form of consecration is the charging of an object by sacrifices offered to it. This method is common throughout the world. As a rule, animals are killed in such a consecration and their life force is channeled into the object.

This method is, of course, extremely brutal from the point of view of today's vegetarians, but it should be remembered that it probably dates back to a time when people lived to a large extent from hunting and the killing of animals was therefore something completely commonplace.

The greatest of this kind of sacrifice was the human sacrifice. This version was also once widespread. It was most extremely common among the Aztecs, who fought a "flower war" every year to get enough captives for their human sacrifices.

Some Indian tribes in North America, such as the Dakotas, hold that only one's own blood is a true sacrifice, since there is nothing else that really belongs to oneself.

In "consecration by sacrifice," the entire life force of the victim is transferred to the object to be consecrated. This object does not thereby become the secondary body of, for example, the deity whose statue is consecrated in this way, but the life force of the victim transferred to the statue makes the statue alive, habitable, and inviting to the deity.

IV 5.   Further contexts

In connection with these various methods of consecration, there are some related phenomena which are worth considering, as they make the process of consecration still clearer.

IV 5. a)   Consecration and Trauma

In a consecration, vital force is bound to an object. One can also say that the object is linked to a consciousness content – this consciousness content can be in the psyche of an individual (image) or in the collective subconsciousness (archetype, deity). This life force is fixed in the object.

Such fixation of life force is also found in other places. For example, in slaughterhouses, prisons, torture chambers, trenches, concentration camps, and the like, there is a strong bond between the extreme feelings that people have experienced there and the place itself, which then takes on this quality. These qualities can then often be perceived by people in these places even after a long time. The place has become a magical place as a result of the event – albeit with an evil quality.

One can compare this process with a trauma in the psyche of a person. A trauma occurs when a person experiences something existentially threatening and immediatly afterwards has no way of releasing the maximum inner tension that arose during this experience. In such a case, the feelings that the person experienced in the extreme situation become fixed and become, so to speak, a canned emotion in the basement of the psyche of this person.

The above examples of imprinting of a place by torture and the like can also be understood as traumas that have been fixed not only in a person but also in a place. Such imprints of a place are often difficult to dissolve – this form of "consecration" of a place may not have been intended, but is nevertheless very effective.

In the formation of a trauma, there is a "one-directedness by need" in the psyche of the person concerned; in normal magic, on the other hand, there is a "one-directedness by intention". However, the effect of these two very different forms of one-directedness is the same: effective magic.

IV 5. b)   Crop circles

When you enter a fresh crop circle that has just been created, you immediately feel a great force that is like an electric tingle, like a field of tension that you are entering, like a transition into a realm with a completely different quality. This "magic charge" of a fresh crop circle is so strong that it is also perceived by many untrained people who do not expect such a phenomenon at all.

Consequently, a crop circle is also a magical object – whereby the view about the one who "consecrated" this crop circle depends on which view one has about the formation of crop circles. For myself, the collective subconsciousness seems to be the most probable originator – what else should be able to accomplish such a degree of telekinesis that sometimes over a length of more than 100 meters, crop stalks bend in a perfect symmetry without breaking them?

IV 5. c)   Aura reading

There is the possibility of inwardly aligning oneself with a person, an object, or a place, and then looking at the condition and past history of that object, person, or place. This works largely exactly the same as dream travel.

This way of obtaining information is sometimes called "psychometry".

This possibility shows that the history of an object or being remains connected with this place and is also perceptible for outsiders. So every object and being has an inside which contains the history of this object or being. If this history is also perceptible to outsiders, this means that there is the possibility to temporarily couple the consciousness of an observer to the consciousness ("inside") of any object or being.

This process is ultimately the same as what happens in a consecration: A certain content of consciousness is attached to an object or a being – in the case of consecration, however, ideally permanently.

Obviously, the production of consecrated magical objects (and also a large part of other magic) can be understood as the production of links from an object or being to external contents of consciousness.

IV 5. d) Consecration and Homeopathy

The description of the production of magical objects can also be used to describe the mode of action of homeopathy.

In homeopathy, a substance such as sulfur is thoroughly mixed with lactose in a fixed ratio (e.g. 1:10) – this mixture would then be called "D1" (D = deka = 10). This mixing is then repeated again and again with the same mixing ratio. Thus, the sulfur in a "D4" potency would then only be contained in a mixing ratio of 1:10,000. In the "C" potencies, the mixing ratio is 1:100 (C = centum = 100). A "C4" potency contains the sulfur only in a mixing ratio of 1:100,000,000.

This continual mixing results in less and less of the sulfur being in the mixture – until finally the sulfur is no longer detectable. By this trick one obtains a substance in which the sulfur is no longer contained as matter, but only as life force. The mixture, which chemically is finally only milk sugar, has nevertheless been shaped by the sulfur. This is a special kind of consecreation.

By this procedure one achieves that by the ingestion of a homoeopathic globule the vital force effect of the sulfur is set in motion, but that one does not cause any chemical-biological reactions to sulfur, since in the globule no sulfur is contained any more.

In homeopathy, therefore, lactose is used as a substance that is magically imprinted by mixing. Therefore the globules are magically effective objects: they connect the one who takes them with the consciousness of the substance from which the globules have been made – in the example used here with the "spirit of sulfur".

What is interesting about this method is that it works without the concentration and imagination of the one who mixes the original substance with the lactose. The mixing itself is sufficient. This is reminiscent of Feng Shui, the effect of repetition, the effect of wearing a ring for a long time on that ring, and similar processes.

Magic apparently does not depend on a person consciously practicing it. This can be seen, among other things, in the fact that astrology works reliably and shapes all events (transits) including a person's lifestyle (horoscope).

This is a magic aspect that should be taken into account when making magic objects.

The symbols (including deities and temples), the homeopathic beads and the orgone accumulator are the three things that have a magical effect on their own, without the need for a person to create this effect through imagination and concentration. One can describe this effect most simply as a connection to a spirit or to a deity – that is, as the connecting of the magical object to a certain consciousness.

IV 5. e)   Consecration and Politics

Most politicians, like the military, are pragmatists – they use what works. Politicians also use the possibility of imprinting places and then, through this detour, directing the people who are in those places.

Demagogues have always appreciated large buildings as well as marches and dramatic performances: from the games in the Colosseum in Rome to the mass human sacrifices in the Aztec temples to the mass events of the Nazis.

It is often difficult to judge how much conscious magical imprint is in each of these ritual-like events – but it worked …

IV 5. f)   Symbolism and Intention

In the consecrations and the productions of magical objects it has been shown that there is a certain hierarchy of influences:

- The chosen symbolism apparently ultimately prevails over all other influences. It is therefore of great importance that when making a magical object, one carefully examines what it is supposed to do and be able to do, and which symbolism is therefore best suited to it.

- The motivation, concentration and imagination of the one who performs the consecration and possibly also the making of the object is of great importance. However, since the intensity and clarity of these three inner activities can vary greatly, their influence cannot be defined in general terms – but the more, the better. However, a wrong symbolism cannot be corrected by an intense imagination.

- The substances from which the object is made give the "color", so to speak, to the imprint. They do not determine what effect the object has, but at least in what way it acts: silver – soft; iron – hard; amber – organic, etc.

- The ritual by which the object is consecrated directs the power in a certain direction. Therefore, the ritual is an aspect of motivation, concentration and imagination.

- The place and time of the consecration determine the birth chart of the magical object and thus shape its character. This effect is similar to that of the material from which the object has been made: for example, the symbolism determines that the object is like a bear, but the horoscope may determine that this bear is sociable like a Libra (if the ascendant of the horoscope of the magic object is in Libra).

IV 5. g)   The unintended consecration

There are also consecrations that are unintended. Of these consecrations, among others, the imprinting of jewelry by years of wearing by the same person and the imprinting of places by the events at them have already been mentioned.

There is still another aspect with this topic, which was examined so far however quite rarely: Does an object develop, if it becomes ever more complex, a psyche? And can it therefore react faster and eventually become active itself?

These questions arise above all in the case of PCs and the Internet. If they begin to develop a psyche themselves due to their complexity, they approach the status of a living being. It is at least generally known by now that PCs react much more sensitively to stress than e.g. a table, which remains still even under great stress of the people sitting at it. PCs, on the other hand, can crash, they can start automatically, the processor can burn out and many other things.

This does not have to mean that a PC is a magical object with a consciousness that enables the PC to be aware of itself – but the question of what actually happens in PCs on the level of life force and consciousness is worthwhile: On the one hand, all things have a consciousness side, and if the material side is as complex as in a PC, the consciousness side will also contain complex structures. On the other hand, the reactions of PCs to human stress could also be explained by human telekinesis.

Sometimes PCs do things which are difficult to explain. For example, about 15 years ago, when I started my own business as an author and counsellor, I applied for foundation support. When I stood with all my documents in front of the office of the person in charge before the final meeting, I felt quite queasy – would it all work out or not? The whole further course of my life depended on it …

Finally, I realized how nervous I was. Then I told myself that I had learned magic after all and consequently I collected myself, checked my goal once again and found it to be right. Then I let my heart chakra shine and simply anchored myself in the "I am I". After a short time I felt like a little sun and was looking forward to the upcoming meeting.

Then, when I had entered and sat down, the clerk opened my case in her PC. She looked at her screen with a wrinkled forehead, typed for a while and finally said to me that my case had already been approved, although I had not yet submitted my documents, and that she also had no access to this approval and could not reverse it – and that everything could not actually be the way it was.

What else could she do than to approve the foundation support for me?

Was this a case of unconscious but advanced and precise telekinesis of mine, with which I reprogrammed the PC? Was it a meaningful coincidence that cannot be explained further? Or did the central PC of the Bonn Employment Agency think that I deserved this foundation support?

IV 5. h) Poltergeists and haunted houses

Finally, there is one last case that is worth considering in these contexts: haunted houses. Of course, this is only a topic worth thinking about if you have experienced such a haunting yourself.

Since for a while I was often called to houses that were haunted, I have heard and sometimes witnessed some phenomena: footsteps on the stairs where no one can be seen; invisible people speaking to you; invisible people pulling the covers off your bed; a fierce noise in a room where, when you look, there is no one – it sometimes sounds as if someone is smashing the furniture with an axe; and so on.

There are quite certainly two different causes of these phenomena: stress of residents and the restless spirits of the deceased.

The stress of occupants occurs mainly during puberty – I myself worried my parents' house in this way for half a year with a poltergeist. This poltergeist was the stress in my psyche, which is why the most violent phenomena also occurred in my room (when I was not in there).

Similar violent phenomena occurred in a house in the Bergisches Land. After I tried in vain for a long time to find out who could be the ghost causing the phenomena in this house, it turned out that the daughter of the woman who owned the house had a relationship with her stepfather, i.e. with the woman's new husband. So these were not ghost phenomena, but poltergeist phenomena, caused by the stress especially of the daughter.

In a residential house in Alfter it began to haunt after the owner had died, who in his last ten years of life had only his house, which he rented out, as his purpose in life. After I contacted his ghost, I was able to make him realize that he had died – the ghost of the former landlord was in a kind of half-sleep and had not yet realized that he was dead. After my "dream journey conversation" with him, the haunting phenomena in the house stopped.

In the Alfter castle, where about 40 students lived at that time, there were very probably both kinds of haunting causes – on the one hand the ghosts of two students who had committed suicide in the castle, and a rather conscious and very old ghost who had been walking around there probably for hundreds of years, and on the other hand also the psychic stress of the students who lived there. For sending the spirits to the other world I got an acquaintance to help me – they were too many and too strong spirits for one person …

Is a haunted house or castle also a magical object? At least the haunting phenomena are very similar to the properties and abilities of a magical object.

IV 6. The effect

One essential question has not yet been considered: What properties can a magical object acquire? What is such an object capable of? What can a magician or a witch achieve with such an object that she could not achieve without it?

IV 6. a) Myths and magical objects

First of all, it can be stated that magical objects with extraordinary properties appear mainly in fantasy novels. However, they can also be found in some myths. Interestingly, in myths these objects almost always belong to the gods. Sometimes the gods give these items to the heroes, who are often the sons of these gods.

The magical objects generally seem to originate from the gods and illustrated in former times certain aspects of the myths of these gods. In some cases, the heroes in the myths and legends or the people in the cult then tried to make these gods' objects themselves. In this way the magic sword, the immortality potion, the invisibility cloak, the winged shoes, the infallible arrow, the magic cauldron etc. were created.

These gods' objects are therefore the archetypes of the magical objects made by man. Both the origin of these archetypes and the attempts to create them as concrete magical objects themselves are a complex matter.

For example, the invisibility cloak, the winged shoes, the witch's broom, and the flying carpet are all illustrations of astral journeys: The astral body is invisible and can fly.

The attempt to produce the immortality potion, which was originally the milk of the mother goddess in the afterlife, as a concrete drink, has led to the emergence of alchemy. A motive that developed along the way is the vessel for this potion, which is, among other things, the root of the legend of the Holy Grail.

However, the emergence of ideas about certain magical objects does not yet help to identify what is actually possible.

IV 6. b) Known magical properties

If you take a look around at what special magical objects can be found nowadays, you can already discover some things that are quite interesting:

- Magical objects sometimes feel like a living body and seem to be filled with a pulsating warmth.
This is described quite vividly in the last book of the "Harry Potter"-series as the warmth, the pulsation and the radiation of the "horcruxes".

- Both temples and statues can have such an intense radiance that it makes your hair stand on end.

- Some statues are reported to have moved, to have tears running down their faces, and so on. I have not experienced such things myself, but since such phenomena are found in such different traditions as Christianity, Germanic religion and Central American shamans, and I have also been told such experiences by trustworthy magic colleagues, it seems to me to be reasonable to assume the existence of such phenomena.
After all, such phenomena are not much different from the events at telekinesis experiments and in haunted houses, which I know well enough.

- Magical objects can have distinctive properties. For example, the snake rings I forged had the peculiarity that everything I wished for when I wore such a ring came true rather quickly.

- A Spiritus familiaris can carry out orders quite effectively – involve a certain person in an accident, get a certain out-of-print book, protect a place, etc.

- The homeopathic globules are magical objects that have very precise effects.

- A statue of Horus can help against scorpion stings. The effect of the water poured over such a statue is very similar to the effect of the homeopathic globules.

- A voodoo doll is constructed differently and is usually a harming spell, but the basic principle is much the same as with the Horus statue and with the homeopathic globules.

- Crop circles are also magical objects, even though they were not created by a single human being, nor do they have a specific effect.

- By energetic Feng Shui, very precise changes are made to the qualities of a place.

- There are clearly recognizable places of power.

- In a sweat lodge, a certain mood is created when the sweat lodge fire is lit. At this time, various spirits come without being explicitly summoned.

Summarizing these observations, the following characteristics of magical objects emerge:

- They often feel alive and warm sometimes you can feel a pulsation in them (rings, spiritus familiaris, power places).

- The power in them can be so intense that one's hair stands on end or one spontaneously recoils (temples, statues, crop circles).

- They can move out of themselves (statues, deity symbols).

- They can fulfill wishes you tell them (rings, spiritus familiaris).

- They sometimes have very special effects (homeopathic globules, Horus statue, voodoo dolls, energetic Feng Shui).

- There are automatic reactions (sweat lodge).

Summarizing these six points, the image emerges that magical objects behave like living beings: They contain life force, feel alive and vibrant, can act, bring about events, and have special properties and habits.

The conception of a magical object as an artificially produced living being ("golem") thus fits quite well with the observable phenomena.

In the descriptions given here, it should be noted that "life force" is not a strange "magic substance", but the boundary between consciousness and matter. This means that the magical objects are associated with an unusually high degree of consciousness for an object – thus they feel alive and can sometimes act like a living being.

This observation suggests that when an object is consecrated, its chakras should be imagined, since the chakras are the basic structure of the life force. However, I am not aware of any experiments with this approach – except for mentions in novels and movies such as the "Elder Wand" in the "Harry Potter" movies, which has seven nodes, or the wand of Apollonius of Thyana, which also has seven such nodes in the novel about him.

IV 6. c)   Well-known magical objects

Next, we can see what magical objects can be found that are known to have actually existed and to have had special properties.

First of all, you can find the statues of the gods and the temples, as well as some places of power.

Special wands, magic swords, healing chalices and the like, on the other hand, seem to appear only in myths, legends and in fantasy novels. Sometimes there are even lists of such items, such as the "Sanctuaries of Britain" derived from Celtic lore – but these items do not exist as concrete objects that one could actually possess and use.

There are, of course, plenty of consecrated items such as wands, communion cups, vajras, and the like, but there are no known objects that stand out for their exceptionally great power – and which are therefore something that all magicians and witches would fight over possessing.

There are, after all, some statues of gods in which the deity in question is so present that it occasionally performs a miracle, moves, or does something else extraordinary. These statues, however, do not evoke the possessiveness that is so typical in fantasy novels regarding magical objects.

IV 6. d)   The size of the effect

The magnitude of the effect a magic object can have is not as easy to describe as it may seem at first glance – the situations are usually quite complex …

> - With the homeopathic beads you can possibly cure a disease that would have led to death if not cured. Can this be increased? But isn't the taking of homeopathic glubules completely unspectacular?
>
> The same applies to the healing of scorpion bites by water poured over a statue of Horus.
>
> The counterpart to this healing method would be murder with the help of a voodoo doll.

A bit smaller smaller, but still considerable, is the bringing about of meaningful coincidences e.g. by a Spiritus familiaris.

- One can also measure the size of an effect by how much it contradicts the laws of physics. There the movement of a statue would be a striking case.

- Finally, the distinctive character of an object such as a statue, a temple, or homeopathic globules can be taken as a great effect.

Such things as the phenomena known from fantasy novels, such as the rays of light emitted by magic wands, are searched for in vain in reality – as far as I know.

IV 6. e)   The possibilities of magical objects

Finally, the question remains, what can a magician achieve with such a magical object that he could not achieve without it?

For this, one can once again look into the lore and check whether magic objects appear somewhere, which the people who performed miracles indispensably needed for their extraordinary magic. Such a case does not seem to exist. The men and women about whom miracles are reported, did it all without the help of special objects and also without special rituals – just like that …

This means that while magical objects can be of help, their possession alone cannot be the basis for extraordinary magic.

IV 7. The Structure of a Consecration

Even if the last section has shown that the effect of magic objects is limited (especially compared to such items in fantasy novels), they can still be useful here and there. So, it is worth to describe the creation of such items once as generally as possible, but at the same time precisely.

The first point to clarify is the motivation: What do you want? Is this already the actual goal or just a step towards it? What do you want to achieve in the end?

The most important point in the implementation, according to the previous considerations, is the right symbolism, because it prevails over all other elements in the creation of a magical object.

Therefore, it is best to have sufficient expertise in symbols and myths.

It is interesting to note that there are some effective consecrations that consist only of a very simple symbolism and an equally simple connection, such as the production of homeopathic globules. When an object is successfully connected to a consciousness, this object becomes magical, i.e. it follows in its behavior the consciousness in question.

In the case of homeopathic globules, this connection is most often made to an animal, plant or mineral – then the consciousness to which the globules are connected is the animal mother goddess, the plant elf or the mineral dwarf.

In the case of a statue, a temple, most talismans and the like, the consciousness to which a connection is made is a deity.

With most magic objects there is a ritual consecration, i.e. the summoning of life force or a deity, a planet, an element, a spirit or the like. This invocation is, so to speak, an "invocation into the object". It requires concentration and imagination.

During the construction of such a ritual one can become quite creative and look, which symbolisms, myths etc. could promote the magic coinage of the object. Then one puts all these elements together in a meaningful order, which should ideally contain an arc of tension and lead from the general to the specific: e.g. first an invocation of fire, then an invocation of the planet Mars and finally an invocation of the Greek god of war Ares.

If there is a traditional form of invocation of a specific object such as a vajra, one should use that invocation – it will likely be very effective.

The same is true for ancient invocations, hymns to gods, spells, pyramid texts and the like. As a rule, these texts are effective because their great age means that they have been read and used many times and thus have a great "resonance".

Repeating the consecration can also be beneficial, e.g. calling daily Fire, Mars and Ares into a statue of Ares – or Air, Mercury and Hermes into a statue of Hermes – or Water, Moon and Isis into a statue of Isis, etc.

If the intimacy and intensity of the invocation is great, it does not matter so much what one has chosen as an object. In Tibet, it is said quite aptly, "By worship, even a dog bone can be made to glow."

Since there are very many different things that could be made into magical objects, there is ultimately no universal recipe for consecration.

With a statue, the invocation is ultimately most important – preferably with a group of people now and then. Also inner conversations with this deity, dream journeys to it, family constellations with it as a theme and the like can promote the "magical charge" of a statue.

In the case of a temple, one will probably in almost all cases pronounce and imagine the different parts of the temple and their symbolism, invoking and asking for support from the deities that may be associated with that part of the temple.

In the case of a talisman, the focus is also on invoking the deity to give strength to the wish expressed by the talisman.

Some magical objects such as the torque (otherworld journey ring) of the Celts and Germanic tribes have fallen out of fashion because they have been more a sign of the otherworld journey (astral journey) experienced than something that has an effect itself. The same is true of the magic wand, which is essentially the symbol of the connection to the gods, but does not itself establish that connection.

- - -

Finally, the point of the connection of consciousness, which has already been mentioned several times, is the most important: A statue of the Egyptian lion goddess Sakhmet, into which the goddess Sakhmet has been invoked over a long period of time, receives an emanation which is not to be misunderstood.

The greater and more comprehensive the consciousness is that takes over the consecrated object as a body, the greater becomes the power of this object and the more it can effect.

A statue of Mary at a pilgrimage site is so often seen as a "gateway to Mary" that this statue eventually becomes so intensely connected with the "goddess" Mary that this statue (i.e. Mary, who has taken this statue as her body) also fulfills the requests that are addressed to her.

The same is true of Pan statues, Freyr statues, Amaterasu statues, Quetzalcoatl statues, etc. The important point is that such a statue is not just a piece of metal, clay or wood, but it becomes an "inhabited statue" when someone invokes the deity in question into that statue often and intensely enough.

IV 8.   Risks and Side Effects

There are definitely risks and side effects involved in the production of magical objects. These arise mainly from improper procedures. This can best be explained by some examples.

IV 8. a)   The Spiritus familiaris

One of the most serious problems arises when one uses one's own life force to charge a magical object – as is the case with a Spiritus familiaris.

Since life force is not a "magical substance" but simply the direct perception of matter by one's consciousness, by charging a statuette with one's life force one extends one's consciousness to the statuette – one makes the statuette a part of one's own body.

This is the same process as in hypnosis, where one also extends one's own consciousness to the body of another person. Also in telepathy and telekinesis there is this expansion of consciousness. However, the expansion of consciousness to a Spiritus familiaris is meant to be permanent and not temporary as in telepathy, telekinesis and hypnosis. One creates oneself an additional third arm by a Spiritus familiaris, so to speak.

If a part of one's own consciousness is permanently no longer in one's own body, but in the statuette of the Spiritus familiaris, this part of one's own consciousness naturally separates itself from the rest of consciousness over time, becomes more independent and develops its own dynamics. Of course, this does not have to lead to schizophrenia, but it can become a trouble spot in one's own consciousness.

If one then decides to dissolve this Spiritus familiaris again, it can feel as if one would kill a beloved pet or as if one would amputate one's own arm.

The permanent extension of one's own consciousness to an object or the permanent transfer of a part of one's own consciousness to an object can lead to difficulties, because one finally experiences this object as a part of one's own body. Then dependency-phenomena may well occur.

In the course of time this Spiritus familiaris may become more and more independent. Then one has to destroy this ghost. That can be experienced like an amputation of one' left arm.

IV 8. b)   The Snake Rings

The same as for a Spiritus familiaris also applies to other objects which one has intentionally or unintentionally charged with one's own life force – to which one has thus extended one's own consciousness and thus made them a part of one's own body. Also the melting down of the already mentioned snake rings was connected with a very intensive feeling of self-amputation and self-mutilation.

The feeling of dependence on an object and addiction to it is, after all, described in detail and rather aptly in "The Lord of the Rings" …

The second problem that arose in connection with the snake rings was the inappropriate symbolism of the rings:

> 1. The problem was the dying of the forest due to acid rain. However, the forest did not need more power to withstand the acid rain, but less sulfur in the exhaust gases so that the rain would no longer be acidic.

> 2. The snakes symbolize the strength of the earth – in this respect they fit to the idea to want to strengthen the forest (even if the forest needed in reality less sulfur). However, I forged the snake rings as closed rings – they bit themselves in the tail and were therefore trapped and not free. Thus I called with the rings the imprisoned snake power and not the free snake power.

> 3. I forged twelve rings with a tourmaline on the snake's head and a larger, thirteenth ring with a ruby on the snake's head to be buried in the center of Germany on the Vogelsberg. However, I have always kept this thirteenth ring with me and I have often worn one of the twelve rings instead of burying it in its place. And I never noticed the great similarities with the rings in the "Lord of the Rings" …

> 4. If I had looked more closely at my feelings for these rings even once, I would have noticed that they were connected with my feeling of always being the victim, and moreover also with my sexuality, which at that time was rather massively repressed. The closed snake ring, i.e. the symbolism of the imprisoned snake power, fit this very precisely.

So the snake rings were on the one hand the wrong medicine for the sickness of the forest, on the other hand a wrongly produced medicine (the wrong symbolism), and thirdly still connected in an intensive way both with the shadow sides of my own psyche and with generally known myths ("Lord of the Rings"). So they could not work.

The next problem arose when the first people undertook dream journeys to these rings and met beings who did not seem helpful at all, but rather extremely dominant. Since the rings unconsciously also served to compensate for my own feelings of powerlessness, it was logical that these rings attracted beings who were power-hungry. And Sauron, the "Lord of the Rings", has become an archetype for an extremely dominant being.

After several people confirmed this perception of dominant beings that had been associated with the Rings, a large part of the people involved in the Rings project decided that the Rings must be destroyed. As you might expect from the descriptions in The Lord of the Rings, I resisted this tooth and nail for a long time. But finally I gave in and agreed.

However, the rings had become so strong in the meantime that they also resisted their destruction themselves – this is also well known from the "Lord of the Rings". On the way to one of the rings by car, a car tire disintegrated on the highway, but this was noticed just in time before the tire burst. On the way to a ring place, in the absence of wind, a huge tree suddenly fell in front of the group that was going there. There were more similar events.

When I finally had all thirteen rings lying on my forge table and melted them down (like Frodo in Mount Doom), it was like cutting off an arm and losing all my power. I was so distraught at the time that I just threw the lump of silver with the twelve tourmalines and the one ruby in it down the toilet and flushed it. But a quarter of an hour later one of my sisters came by and gave me this nugget of silver, saying that she had found it on the floor of the bathroom and that it must have fallen out of my pocket.

So I rode my bike to the Rhine and sank it into the Rhine from the Rhine bridge – from where it never came back to me. I was not aware at that time that the Nibelungen hoard at the Loreley rock had also been sunk into the Rhine and that the most valuable thing in this hoard had been the ring of Tyr-Hreidmar and Loki. Apparently, I was also still resonating with the Germanic myths, which are, after all, the roots of Tolkien's "Lord of the Rings".

The only good thing that can be said about this whole Ring story is that it taught me a lot about magic. Afterwards, I decided to first study all the old myths and symbolism very thoroughly, so that something like this would not happen to me again.

Such a large expenditure, which led then in the long run to nothing, one should avoid if possible …

IV 8. c)   The Temple

Another kind of problem can occur when talismans are made incorrectly or the wishes associated with them are formulated incorrectly. For example, if you make a Jupiter talisman out of pewter because you want to find a temple, it may be that you have misjudged the need of the participants for a temple, that the participants cannot finance it at all, that some participants have dropped out again, that the rental contract runs for a very long time, etc.

This kind of problem can be avoided if one does not choose a very precise formulation for talismans (and also in general in magic), but a more general formulation carried by self-love, which wishes for the best and most suitable. The important point here is being borne by self-love – if this is the motivation, the result of the magic will also be something that can be enjoyed from the heart.

IV 8. d)   The homeopathic remedy test

In homeopathy, knowledge of the action of the various globules is gained by taking a previously unused substance and making globules from it – for example, from the chemical element bismuth. Then several homeopaths take these globules at a working meeting and over several days note down everything they notice – dreams, events, physical complaints, social occurrences, etc. This is then compiled and afterwards summarized.

This remedy description is then used to see if a patient has exactly the symptoms that appeared in the bismuth remedy test. If so, that patient is given homeopathic bismuth globules to further his healing.

When testing a previously unknown remedy, as in this example of bismuth, the examiners experience all the symptoms that can then later be cured in the patient by this remedy. So the testers swallow a magic object unknown to them (here the bismuth globules) and wait to see what will happen. Quite brave …

This can sometimes lead to prolonged illnesses, physical ailments, altered psychological or social behaviors such as irascibility or jealousy. Then the examiners suddenly find themselves in the middle of Goethe's "Sorcerer's Apprentice": they can no longer get rid of the ghosts they have summoned – at least not quickly. Sometimes the symptoms caused by taking the globules soon subside soon, but sometimes one has to deal with the after-effects for several years.

IV 8. e)   Harm Spells

Damage spells also use magical objects – the best known of them is certainly the voodoo doll.

However, there are other methods as well, such as the note with the curse, which is hidden under the doorstep of an enemy.

Then there are also some methods used to make other people dependent – especially in intended relationships. In this case, an intense connection is often established by the magician giving the woman some of his semen to eat hidden in a dish, or by the witch giving the man some of her menstrual blood to eat hidden in a dish.

In these methods, a connection between two people is established each time, which ultimately serves to make it easier for the magician or the witch to extend their consciousness to the other person and to make the other do what the magician or the witch wants. So, the above methods can also be considered as hypnosis aids.

These methods have two disadvantages:

- On the one hand, by using methods in which one exerts coercion on others, one reinforces in oneself the basic feeling of lack, which can only be (temporarily) filled by power and force – but which ultimately only reinforces the actual problem.

- On the other hand, the victim, if he also knows something about magic or gets expert help, can now, with the help of the magical connection that was previously established by the magician or the witch, for his part quite easily proceed to a counterattack.

IV 8. f)   The unexpectedly great effect

The effect of a Spiritus familiaris cannot necessarily be dosed precisely – if you are angry with someone and then send the Spiritus familiaris on him with the most evil wishes, it can happen that after a while you learn that the person concerned had a car accident, that his wife has separated from him, that his company has gone bankrupt and that he has been diagnosed with an incurable cancer. Then you stand there and can ask yourself if that was exactly what you wanted – and if you actually caused all of that, or if some of it would have happened without your doing …

Of course, such devastating effects do not always have to occur when one sends out a Spiritus familiaris or when one pronounces a formal curse and attaches it to an "enemy" with the help of an object – but it happens all the time.

Ideally, this should be considered beforehand.

V The necessity of magic objects

After all these considerations, the question of whether you actually need magic objects naturally arises.

Some magical objects, such as statues and temples, are extremely useful and facilitate the common ritual and contact with a deity (especially for the untrained).

Then there are also people for whom it has proven practical to create a symbol for each spirit and god with whom they have contact, which is then a gateway to that being. That would be then the procedure of a fetish priest. The counterpart would be the Hindu or Buddhist yogi who sits on the edge of the forest and meditates without any possessions.

For most people, an attitude somewhere between the fetish priest and the property-less yogi is the appropriate one. Where exactly this fitting place is, everyone has to find out for himself – maybe it differs from situation to situation.

In general one can say that there is no spell for which you absolutely need a magic object – but on the other hand there is probably no spell for which you could use no magic objects at all. They are neither indispensable nor useless, but simply tools that you can use if you want to.

As with so many things, it is ultimately a matter of personal style as to how one proceeds and whether one uses magic items in the process.

In magic, on the one hand, the expansion of one's own consciousness to another being/object and, on the other hand, the establishment of a connection to a spirit/god are the basic methods of influence. Therefore, objects that have been connected to a spirit or a deity play a role in magic again and again.

However, these magic objects are always only aids. What is actually active is the acting human being or the spirit or the deity – who may have extended their consciousness to an object.

English Books by Harry Eilenstein

- Living Magic (261 p.)
- The Synthesis of Physics and Magic (192 p.)
- Astral Projection for Beginners (60 p.)
- Invocations for Beginners (52 p.)
- Evocations for Beginners (62 p.)
- Auto-Movement for Beginners (60 p.)
- Elves for Beginners (56 p.)
- Hypnosis for Beginners (56 p.)
- Money Magic for Beginners (60 p.)
- Magic Objects for Beginners (64 p.)
- Shamanism for Beginners (52 p.)
- Crop Circles for Beginners (344 p.)
- Number Symbolism for Beginners (64 p.)

These books will be puplished soon:

- Telepathy for Beginners
- Telepathy for Advanced Learners
- Telekinesis for Beginners
- Life Force for Beginners

- Meditation for Beginners
- Kundalini for Beginners
- Chakra-Magic for Beginners
- Astrology for Beginners
- Ritual Magic for Beginners
- Mandalas for Beginners
- Love Magic for Beginners
- Magic Research for Beginners
- Self-awareness for Beginners
- Symbolism of Numbers for Beginners
- Language of the Moon – for Beginners
- Magic Chant for Beginners
- Prophecy for Beginners
- Da'ath-Magic for Beginners
- Feng Shui for Beginners
- Magic for Beginners – Anthology I
- Magic for Beginners – Anthology II
- Magic for Beginners – Anthology III
- Magic for Beginners – Anthology IV

Bücher von Harry Eilenstein

Religion allgemein
- Die sieben Schritte des Lebens (428 S.)
- Muttergöttin und Schamanen (168 S.)
- Göbekli Tepe (472 S.)
- Die Göttin von Göbekli Tepe (144 S.)
- Totempfähle (440 S.)
- Christus (60 S.)
- Dakini (80 S.)
- Vajra (76 S.)

Ägypten
- Hathor und Re 1: Götter und Mythen im Alten Ägypten (432 S.)
- Hathor und Re 2: Die altägyptische Religion – Ursprünge, Kult und Magie (396 S.)
- Isis (508 S.)

Indogermanen
- Die Entwicklung der indogermanischen Religionen (700 S.)
- Wurzeln und Zweige der indogermanischen Religion (224 S.)

Germanen
- Die Götter der Germanen (87 Bände – siehe nächste Seite)
- Odin (300 S.)

Kelten
- Cernunnos (690 S.)
- Taliesin (228 S.)
- Der Kessel von Gundestrup (220 S.)
- Der Chiemsee-Kessel (76)

Psychologie
- Über die Freude (100 S.)
- Das Geheimnis des inneren Friedens (252 S.)
- Das Beziehungsmandala (52 S.)
- Gefühle und ihre Verwandlungen (404 S.)
- einsgerichtet (140 S.)
- Liebe und Eigenständigkeit (216 S.)
- Von innerer Fülle zu äußerem Gedeihen (52 S.)

Heilung
- Die Symbolik der Krankheiten (76 S.)

Kunst
- Herz des Tanzes – Tanz des Herzens (160 S.)

Drama
- König Athelstan (104 S.)

Bücher von Harry Eilenstein

„Magie für Anfänger"

- Telepathie für Anfänger (60 S.)
- Telepathie für Fortgeschrittene (52 S.)
- Telekinese für Anfänger (52 S.)
- Lebenskraft für Anfänger (60 S.)
- Meditation für Anfänger (56 S.)
- Kundalini für Anfänger (100 S.)
- Hypnose für Anfänger (56 S.)
- Auto-Movement für Anfänger (56 S.)
- Chakra-Magie für Anfänger (148 S.)
- Astralreisen für Anfänger (56 S.)
- Astrologie für Anfänger (120 S.)
- Ritual-Magie für Anfänger (56 S.)
- Mandalas für Anfänger (68 S.)
- Geldzauber für Anfänger (56 S.)
- Liebeszauber für Anfänger (52 S.)
- Invokationen für Anfänger (52 S.)
- Evokationen für Anfänger (60 S.)
- Elfen für Anfänger (56 S.)
- Magie-Forschung für Anfänger (140 S.)
- Selbsterkenntnis für Anfänger (52 S.)
- Zahlensymbolik für Anfänger (60 S.)
- Die Sprache des Mondes – für Anfänger (116 S.)
- Zaubergesänge für Anfänger (100 S.)
- Zukunftschau für Anfänger (60 S.)
- Schamanismus für Anfänger (52 S.)
- Magische Gegenstände für Anfänger (68 S.)
- Da'ath-Magie für Anfänger (64 S.)
- Kornkreise für Anfänger (348 S.)
- Feng Shui für Anfänger (96 S.)
- Magie für Anfänger – Sammelband I (696 S.)
- Magie für Anfänger – Sammelband II (664 S.)
- Magie für Anfänger – Sammelband III (580 S.)

„Traumreisen"

- Traumreisen zu Heilpflanzen (700 S.)

Magie

- Handbuch für Zauberlehrlinge (408 S.)
- Tarot (104 S.)
- Physik und Magie (184 S.)
- Die Synthese von Physik und Magie (200S.)
- Die Magie-Formel (156 S.)
- Krafttiere – Tiergöttinnen – Tiertänze (112 S.)
- Schwitzhütten (524 S.)
- Mythen und Magie der Harfe (116 S.)
- Magie heute – Berichte aus der Praxis (288 S.)

Meditation

- Der Lebenskraftkörper (230 S.)
- Die Chakren (100 S.)
- Das Chakren-System mit den Nebenchakren (296 S.)
- Organe und Chakren (64 S.)
- Die platonischen Körper in den Chakren (156 S.)
- Meditation (140 S.)
- Drachenfeuer (124 S.)
- Kundalini I (676 S.)
- Reinkarnation (156 S.)
- einsgerichtet (140 S.)

Astrologie

- Astrologie (496 S.)
- Photo-Astrologie (428 S.)
- Die astrologischen Aspekte (88 S.)
- Horoskop und Seele (120 S.)

Kabbala

- Kursus der praktischen Kabbala (150 S.)
- Eltern der Erde (450 S.)
- Blüten des Lebensbaumes:
  - Die Struktur des kabbalistischen Lebensbaumes (370 S.)
  - Der kabbalistische Lebensbaum als Forschungshilfsmittel (580 S.)
  - Der kabbalistische Lebensbaum als spirituelle Landkarte (520 S.)

Die Themen der 87 Bände der Reihe „Die Götter der Germanen"